How To Use Positive Practice, Self-Correction, and Overcorrection

SECOND EDITION

Nathan H. Azrin
and
Victoria A. Besalel

How To Manage Behavior Series

R. Vance Hall
and
Marilyn L. Hall
Series Editors

pro·ed
An International Publisher

8700 Shoal Creek Boulevard
Austin, Texas 78757-6897
800/987-3202 Fax 800/397-7633
www.proedinc.com

D1158444

© 1999, 1982 by PRO-ED, Inc.
8700 Shoal Creek Boulevard
Austin, Texas 78757-6897
800/897-3202   Fax 800/397-7633
www.proedinc.com

Library of Congress Cataloging-in-Publication Data

Azrin, Nathan H., 1930–
    How to use positive practice, self-correction, and overcorrection
/ Nathan H. Azrin and Victoria A. Besalel.—2nd ed.
      p. cm.—(How to manage behavior series)
    Rev. ed. of: How to use overcorrection. 1980, and How to use
positive practice. 1981.
    Includes bibliographical references.
    ISBN-13: 978-089079792-1 (alk. paper)
    ISBN-10: 0-89079-792-7 (alk. paper)
    1. Behavior modification. 2. Behavior modification—Case studies.
I. Besalel-Azrin, Victoria A. II. Azrin, Nathan H., 1930– How to
use overcorrection. III. Azrin, Nathan H., 1930– How to use
positive practice. IV. Title. V. Series.
BF637.B4A97 1999
153.8'5—dc21

98-36536
CIP

This book is designed in Palatino and Frutiger.

Art Director: Thomas Barkley
Designer: Jason Crosier

Printed in the United States of America

7 8 9 10 11   18 17 16 15 14

Contents

Preface to Series

The first edition of the *How To Manage Behavior Series* was launched some 15 years ago in response to a perceived need for teaching aids that could be used by therapists and trainers. The widespread demand for the series has demonstrated the need by therapists and trainers for nontechnical materials for training and treatment aids for parents, teachers, and students. Publication of this revised series includes many updated titles of the original series. In addition, several new titles have been added, largely in response to therapists and trainers who have used the series. A few titles of the original series that proved to be in less demand have been replaced. We hope the new titles will increase the usefulness of the series.

The editors are indebted to Steven Mathews, Vice President of PRO-ED, who was instrumental in the production of the revised series, as was Robert K. Hoyt, Jr. of H & H Enterprises in producing the original version.

These books are designed to teach practitioners, including parents, specific behavioral procedures to use in managing the behaviors of children, students, and other persons whose behavior may be creating disruption or interference at home, at school, or on the job. The books are nontechnical, step-by-step instructional manuals that define the procedure, provide numerous examples, and allow the reader to make oral or written responses.

The exercises in these books are designed to be used under the direction of someone (usually a professional) with a background in the behavioral principles and procedures on which the techniques are based.

The booklets in the series are similar in format but are flexible enough to be adapted to a number of different teaching situations and training environments.

R. Vance Hall, PhD, is Senior Scientist Emeritus of The Bureau of Child Research and Professor Emeritus of Human Development and Family Life and Special Education at the University of Kansas. He was a pioneer in carrying out behavioral research in classrooms and in homes. Marilyn L. Hall, EdD, taught and carried out research in regular and special public school classrooms. While at the University of Kansas, she developed programs for training parents to use systematic behavior change procedures and was a successful behavior therapist specializing in child management and marriage relationships.

vi How To Manage Behavior

As always, we invite your comments, suggestions, and questions. We are always happy to hear of your successes in changing your own behaviors and the behaviors of other persons to make your lives more pleasant, productive, and purposeful.

R. Vance Hall &
Marilyn L. Hall
Series Editors

How To Manage Behavior Series

How To Maintain Behavior

How To Motivate Others Through Feedback

How To Negotiate a Behavioral Contract

How To Plan for Generalization

How To Select Reinforcers

How To Teach Social Skills

How To Teach Through Modeling and Imitation

How To Use Group Contingencies

How To Use Planned Ignoring

How to Use Positive Practice, Self-Correction, and Overcorrection

How To Use Prompts To Initiate Behavior

How To Use Response Cost

How To Use Systematic Attention and Approval

How To Use Time-Out

How To Use Token Economy and Point Systems

Introduction

This book is designed to explain the use of *positive practice, self-correction,* and *overcorrection* to parents and teachers who have responsibility for the care and supervision of young persons. Other users include childcare workers, counselors, and staff members of institutions for young persons with developmental disabilities, retardation, or emotional disturbances. This book is intended to be part of an instructional program supervised by a counselor or professional person who is familiar with positive practice, self-correction, and overcorrection. Exercises and illustrations included in the manual exemplify the use of these procedures. The instructor should review the fill-in information provided by the reader to ensure the reader's proper understanding and use of these procedures. Feedback and discussion about the exercises should be provided by a professional.

Nathan H. Azrin is a professor at the Center for Psychological Studies of Nova Southeastern University in Fort Lauderdale, Florida. After obtaining a doctorate from Harvard, where he studied under B. F. Skinner, Azrin went on to develop new treatment programs for children, adults, couples, mental hospital patients, and the developmentally disabled. Among the many new treatments he developed are the Token Economy method for patients and children, the Job Club program for the unemployed, the Habit Reversal treatment for tic/habit disorders and Tourette Disorder, the Regulated Breathing program for stuttering, the Dry Bed procedure for enuresis, the Reciprocity Counseling program for marital dysfunction and parent–youth problems, and the overcorrection and positive practice strategies for specific behavioral problems. He has received awards for these contributions from the American Psychological Association and the American Psychological Society. In 1977, the Association for the Advancement of Behavior Therapy conferred its Lifetime Achievement Award on him for these new applications.

Victoria A. Besalel received her doctorate from Southern Illinois University and is currently director of the A&B Psychological Clinic. She has been a public school teacher at the elementary and high school levels, and at the university level, she taught special education, child development, and rehabilitation. She has also been a director and teacher of her own nursery school, an instructor at Southern Illinois University, and associate director of the Nova University Psychology Clinic. She has authored many journal studies and books dealing with classroom conduct and achievement, parent–child and parent–youth relations, teaching the developmentally disabled, nocturnal enuresis, marital counseling, vocational counseling and job placement, self-injury and aggression, depression and mood disorders, positive practice and overcorrection, stuttering, compulsive behaviors, and drug abuse by youth and adults. Besalel has been program director of several federal and state funded research projects and is currently active in her independent clinical practice in Fort Lauderdale, Florida.

A list of references at the end of the book includes many of the studies that have used these procedures should the reader or supervisor wish further technical information about these methods. These references also provide a more complete description of specific problems, such as toilet training, classroom management, aggression, stuttering, habit control, bedwetting, stealing, as well as conduct developmental disorders and other problem areas.

This book is a revision of two previous books by this publisher titled *How To Use Positive Practice* and *How To Use Overcorrection*. The references and examples have been updated and the contents of the two books have been combined to include both the positive practice and overcorrection procedures.

Part I. Positive Practice

Introduction to Positive Practice

Positive Practice Versus Simple Practice

Positive practice emphasizes learning through practice. The notion of practice is not new. However, the emphasis here is on practicing a corrected behavior when a mistake has been made. This is more than the practice needed when one first learns a new skill. It means stopping all activities whenever an error occurs, and then carefully performing the correct behavior several times. This systematic, repeated practice when an error occurs ensures that the error will be interrupted, in addition to ensuring that the desired behavior will be emphasized.

Example of Positive Practice

Joan was a fifth grader who repeatedly failed to raise her hand in class to ask for permission to leave her seat or to talk aloud. Joan apparently knew what the proper behavior was, because she previously had raised her hand for permission. Simple practice in the usual manner had been given at the start of the year when the teacher asked all the children to raise their hands at the same time to show they understood the instructions.

But now, Joan repeatedly disrupted the class to talk to other children or to walk around the room while the teacher was speaking. As punishment, the teacher reprimanded Joan and did not allow her to go to recess. The teacher did not enjoy scolding the girl, nor did the teacher feel that the girl should be deprived of her recess period, but there seemed to be few alternatives. Little improvement resulted from the teacher's efforts to give instructions, praise Joan, or ignore the problem. Nor did punishment through scolding and loss of recess eliminate the problem. Joan continued to disrupt the class—even after she had just been deprived of recess.

The teacher decided to try *positive practice*. She discussed with Joan what the new rules would be. Whenever Joan would talk or walk about without permission, the teacher would have her return to her seat and practice raising her hand. The teacher would ask Joan to show how she would raise her hand the next time she wished to leave her seat or talk. When her hand had been raised properly for a few seconds, the teacher would tell Joan she had acted correctly and to lower it. "Now, let's try it again," the teacher said. Then she would require Joan to repeat this practice 5 to 10 times. The teacher spoke calmly to avoid showing anger. The practice would start right after a disruptive behavior began so that the practice interrupted it. From Joan's point of view, it would be easier to raise her hand for permission in the beginning, rather than later spend several minutes doing the positive practice. Because the teacher had explained the procedure to Joan before this new rule began, Joan knew what to expect. She understood and agreed to do the practice.

Within two days, Joan's disruptions were eliminated. She raised her hand before leaving her seat or before talking to other children. On the two occasions when Joan forgot to raise her hand, the positive practice was initiated immediately after each instance. However, on those days when Joan raised her hand on her own, the teacher took great care to call on her immediately to encourage her new behavioral pattern.

Self-Test

1. Did the teacher get angry?   Yes ☐   No ☐
2. Did the child cooperate?   Yes ☐   No ☐
3. Was the child inconvenienced by the practice?   Yes ☐   No ☐
4. Did the child get scolded for her misbehavior?   Yes ☐   No ☐
5. Did the child learn, or relearn, the correct behavior?   Yes ☐   No ☐
6. Was the misbehavior interrupted?   Yes ☐   No ☐

Distinctive Features of Positive Practice

The above example illustrates several distinctive features of positive practice. These are:

- Scolding the child is avoided.
- Punishment by spanking or withdrawing privileges is avoided.
- The teacher or parent need not be angry.
- The emphasis is on positive, not negative, behaviors.
- The misbehavior is interrupted immediately.
- The positive behavior becomes habitual through practice.
- The emphasis is on what to do as a substitute for what not to do.

Insufficient Learning as a Cause of the Problem Behavior

Sometimes the child's mistake is not caused by carelessness, as in the previous example with Joan, who simply forgot to ask for permission. *Lack of learning* is sometimes responsible for problem behaviors. The following example illustrates the use of *positive practice* when the child's problem seems to be caused by insufficient learning.

Example: A Bedwetting Problem

Ralph is a 12-year-old boy who wets his bed every night. His mother and father tried almost everything they knew, including waking him up at night, not letting him drink before bedtime, taking him to the doctor for a physical examination, ignoring the problem without saying anything for months, and scolding and threatening him when they felt he was doing it intentionally. Ralph himself was very distressed and insisted that he did not know how to stop. He very much wanted to stop wetting his bed.

His parents eventually found a solution in a training program in which positive practice was a major procedure. They explained to Ralph that whenever the bed was found wet, Ralph would practice the positive behavior of "jumping out of bed and going to the toilet" where he would stay for a moment. Ralph would then repeat this sequence about 10 times. This practice established the habit of arising from bed at night when he sensed he had to urinate. The result was that Ralph wet his bed only twice during the first week.

After the first accident during that first week, Ralph had performed the "getting-up" positive practice 20 times under his mother's supervision, as they had agreed he should do. He was dry the next night, but just to be sure that the habit was well established, he voluntarily performed the "getting-up" positive practice again the next night without being required to do so. His mother realized how strongly Ralph was motivated to learn a positive way of preventing bedwetting when she saw him initiate the practice on his own. She then praised him enthusiastically.

Two types of positive practice responses are possible regarding bedwetting. The first type is to arise from bed when one has the urge to urinate and that is the type used in the "getting-up" practice. A second positive practice response is to actively inhibit or hold back when the urge to urinate appears. As part of the training, Ralph practiced holding back for as long as he could whenever he had the urge to urinate during the day. This "holding-back" practice increased the ability of his bladder to retain urine, so that he could sleep longer during the night without wetting.

During the second week, Ralph had one bedwetting accident after the two accidents during the first week. Another accident occurred during the third week, and then only one more during the fifth week. After each accident, he did the "getting-up" practice as soon as the accident was discovered, and he did it again before going to bed the next night.

Self-Test

1. What are the two types of positive practice responses to bedwetting?

   a. _____

   b. _____

2. Was the problem caused by (circle one):

   a. deliberate misbehavior

   b. lack of learning

3. Was the child motivated to correct the accidents?

   Yes ☐   No ☐

4. Was the child made to feel threatened or punished by the need to do positive practice?

   Yes ☐   No ☐

5. Was the "getting-up" practice given (circle one):

   a. continuously

   b. only when needed

6. Was positive practice a constructive way to deal with this bedwetting problem?

   Yes ☐   No ☐

   Why? _____

   _____

7. Did the positive practice for bedwetting take time or effort by the child?

   Yes ☐   No ☐

(continues)

8. If the accidents were deliberate, do you think the positive practice requirement would have been effective?

   Yes ☐   No ☐

   What reasons are there for it being effective? _____

   _____

   _____

9. Did Ralph's mother supervise him while he was doing the positive practice?

   Yes ☐   No ☐

10. Did Ralph's parents discuss the reasons and procedure for positive practice
    before they began requiring it?

    Yes ☐   No ☐

The correct answers are: (1) holding back and getting up out of bed; (2) b;
(3) yes; (4) no; (5) b; (6) yes; (7) yes; (8) yes; (9) yes; and (10) yes.

The above example illustrates the application of positive practice when
the child's problem is caused by insufficient learning, rather than by deliberate misbehavior or lack of concern.

Deliberate Misbehavior or Insufficient Learning?

When a child's mistake is deliberate, the child is more likely to object to the
extra effort required by positive practice; but, when insufficient learning is
the cause, the child is more likely to perform the positive practice willingly or
even eagerly in order to learn the correct behavior. When the child realizes
that the problem may be avoided in the future by practicing the positive
behaviors, then the child is more likely to look favorably upon the practice.
Practice is encouraged because no blame is attached to the child. Further-
more, if each step in the process is explained, then practicing each step
becomes meaningful and more likely to be carried out in the future.

Positive practice may be effective because of the inconvenience and
effort it involves, or because it provides additional learning. If the child's
errors are caused by a deliberate action, the extra effort involved in positive
practice will discourage future misbehaviors. But if the misbehavior is the
result of insufficient learning, the child will stop the misbehavior—or error—
because of the intensive practice of the correct behavior.

✎ Self-Test

1. Is it necessary to know whether or not an error is deliberate before using positive practice?

   Yes ☐   No ☐

2. If a child shows annoyance during positive practice, the error is likely to be caused by (circle one):

   a. insufficient learning

   b. a deliberate action

3. If a child enthusiastically performs the positive practice, the error is likely to be caused by (circle one):

   a. insufficient learning

   b. a deliberate action

The correct answers are: (1) no; (2) b; and (3) a.

Not Enough Time for Learning

We often give a child too little help. A child may be given verbal instruction but allowed no practice and no transition period between instruction and accomplishment. The child is expected to perform accurately without practice and to have no deficiency in any part of the behavior. Even the instructions may be too brief.

The positive practice procedure provides practice when it is needed, and only when it is needed, which is after a mistake has been made. If no mistakes are made, the instruction was then probably adequate and no practice is needed.

Carelessness

Positive practice requires time and effort. Consequently, a careless person is encouraged to be more careful in the future. The greater the time and effort required in practicing the correct action whenever a mistake occurs, the less likely it is that the mistake will occur again.

Avoiding Criticism and Punishment

The emphasis in positive practice is on practicing positive behaviors. When a problem occurs, the parent decides what the correct behavior should be and then concentrates on helping the child rehearse that correct behavior.

Positive practice is not criticism, nor is it simple punishment meant to cause distress. The parent should avoid criticizing, scolding, using a harsh tone of voice, using physical punishment, or withdrawing a child's privileges. Instead, the parent should emphasize what action the child should perform correctly in the future.

As part of the emphasis on positive behaviors, the parent must avoid negative language, such as, "Don't slam the door," "Don't yell," "Don't curse," "Don't hit him," "Don't forget your homework," and so on. Instead, the positive action should be stressed, such as, "Do your homework after dinner," "Speak softly," or "Please close the door softly."

Below are listed some other positive statements that parents can use when trying to change a child's behavior. Try to fill in the blank spaces.

Negative Instruction	Versus	Positive Instruction
Don't slam the door.	–	Close the door gently.
Don't curse.	–	Speak nicely.
Stop cluttering.	–	Pick up your clothes.
Stop picking your nose.	–	Use a tissue.
Don't forget to . . .	–	Remember to . . .
Stop running in the mall.	–	Walk next to me.
Don't be out too late.	–	_____
Stop fidgeting.	–	_____
Don't argue with the teacher.	–	_____
Don't be late for school.	–	_____
Don't interrupt me.	–	_____
Don't run around the house.	–	_____

Identifying the Response To Be Practiced

Deciding on the Correct Behavior

One of the first steps in using positive practice is to determine what behavior will be practiced. The practice selected should represent the correct behavior. If any other behavior is selected, then the child will be likely to react to the required positive practice as punishment rather than as a necessary and reasonable learning experience.

 Self-Test: Slamming Doors

Assume that a parent wishes to use positive practice to teach a child to close the door gently as he or she enters the house rather than slamming the door. Check which one of the following behaviors would be positive practice.

1. Have him apologize to the parents for the noise.

   Positive Practice: Yes ☐   No ☐

2. Scold him.

   Positive Practice: Yes ☐   No ☐

3. Have him close the door gently.

   Positive Practice: Yes ☐   No ☐

4. Have him explain why doors should not be slammed.

   Positive Practice: Yes ☐   No ☐

5. Have him empty the trash.

   Positive Practice: Yes ☐   No ☐

In the above example, the correct behavior was (3), to close the door gently. Positive practice would require the child to walk in and out of the house several times, each time closing the door gently under the parent's supervision. This practice would ensure that the child practices the correct behavior. In addition, the time and effort spent in repeatedly walking in and out of the house and closing the door gently would motivate the child to be more careful the next time.

During this practice, the parent might detect some specific reason for the slamming and correct it. The problem might be that the child rushed through the entrance, throwing the door out too far as he entered, in which case the parent could instruct him to open the door only part of the way during the positive practice. Or, the parent might discover during the positive practice that the door's spring is too tightly adjusted for a young child, in which case the spring could be readjusted. The positive practice exercise permits the parent, as well as the child, to discover the reasons for the errors.

Self-Test: Forceful Stealing

Consider a girl with mental disabilities who forcefully takes objects from other children in an institutional setting. Which of the following behaviors would constitute positive practice training for her repeated acts of stealing?

1. Have the child return the object.

   Positive Practice: Yes ☐   No ☐

2. Have the child transferred to another room.

   Positive Practice: Yes ☐   No ☐

3. Have the child clean her room.

   Positive Practice: Yes ☐   No ☐

4. Have the child ask the other child for the object.

   Positive Practice: Yes ☐   No ☐

5. Have the child give five reasons for not stealing.

   Positive Practice: Yes ☐   No ☐

6. Have the child ask an adult for a similar object.

   Positive Practice: Yes ☐   No ☐

In the above example, the correct behavior would be (4), that the child should ask the other child if she could have the object. In implementing the positive practice, the adult supervises as the child repeatedly asks for the object from another child, instructing the child when necessary about what to say and do. This practice ensures that the child knows exactly how to ask politely and effectively for objects. During the practice, the child shows that she has learned and demonstrated what she should do.

On the other hand, the girl would not learn how to properly request objects if procedures were used such as sending her to another room, having her return the object, having her list reasons why she should not steal, or having her clean her room. All of these alternatives would have taken time and effort by the child. But only positive practice would ensure that the child actually learned and demonstrated what she should do in the future.

The importance of selecting the correct response for positive practice may be seen in the next example.

Self-Test: Football Playing Errors
_____

Harold is a 12-year-old boy who has difficulty in the school football games. He runs fast, can tag other players easily, and knows all the plays and passes well. But he frequently drops the football when he tries to catch it. The coach then becomes angry and assigns him 10 laps around the field or 30 push-ups or even takes him out of the game.

What should the coach do, using positive practice as his guide?

_____

_____

_____

_____

The correct answer is that the coach should have Harold practice catching the football over and over again under supervision. Having Harold do 30 push-ups, run 10 laps around the field, or prevent him from playing would annoy Harold. Only the catching practice would teach Harold the correct behavior.

Since the child may require detailed instruction or physical assistance to learn the correct behavior, the parent or teacher should supervise the positive practice closely. Preferably, the parent or teacher should remain next to the child to provide immediate instruction or assistance until the practice trials are being performed correctly and quickly.

Simple Correction Versus Positive Practice

Simple correction may be sufficient when a problem is not severe, has occurred only rarely, or is not a deliberate action to annoy someone. For example, if a child does not pick up the clothes and toys in his or her room, even after repeated reminders, the persistence of this habit suggests that a simple correction or request would not be sufficient. A simple correction might be to have the child interrupt play activity and pick up his or her clothes. For positive practice, the child would be required not only to pick up the clothes once, but to practice picking up the clothes several times, perhaps in each room of the house where the problem has occurred.

The correct response in simple correction is not always the same as the correct response in positive practice. For example, if a child breaks a dish, simple correction would require the child to repair the dish or replace it by paying for or buying another one. But positive practice would require the child to practice the correct manner of handling dishes slowly, gently, and firmly.

When the correct action is different from the positive practice action, both actions can be required. In the above example, the child could be required to practice proper handling of dishes, as well as to replace the broken dish.

Correction is not always possible. In those cases, positive practice can be used. For example, a child who failed to notify the parent that he or she would be late cannot correct that incident, but the child can be given practice in writing notes describing where he or she will be and when he or she will be back. The child should also practice putting notes on the kitchen table before leaving the house.

 ### Self-Test: Vomiting

Another example of the difference between simple correction and positive practice is that of a severely retarded woman who was vomiting on her clothes, in her bed, and in various areas of the ward several times a day. The vomiting appeared to be partly self-induced and deliberate rather than medically related.

What would be a simple correction response that the woman could be required to make?

_____

_____

_____

What would be a positive practice response that the woman could be required to make?

_____

_____

_____

_____

As a correction, the woman might be required to clean up her clothes, bed, and floor area after she vomited. For the positive practice, she might be required to rush to the toilet or sink and bend over it with her mouth open in a "pretend" vomit in the correct place. This practice would be repeated for several trials, each of them initiated from the part of the ward where she had vomited.

In the treatment of this problem, both the correction and positive practice procedures decreased vomiting to zero from a previous average of several episodes per day. The woman spontaneously began rushing to vomit in the toilet stool or sink, without being instructed or requested to do so.

Practicing the Correct Behavior

We have seen that the effectiveness of positive practice depends on the learning taking place and on the time and effort being spent. If only one practice trial is given, then little opportunity is provided for learning to take place, and little time or effort will have been spent. Consequently, positive practice should involve several practice trials. The importance of this can be seen in the following example.

Example: Headweaving

Tina was an 8-year-old autistic girl in a special program. She could not speak and did not learn easily in her individualized instruction. One of the major obstacles to learning was the continuous, side-to-side, rolling movement of her head, which she engaged in at all times. The teachers had repeatedly told her to stop. Then they had tried ignoring it, then rewarding her when she stopped momentarily, and even tried scolding and physically stopping her. But all to no avail. Then positive practice was used.

The first step was to avoid being angry with Tina, which meant that scolding and punishment should not be used. The second step was to identify the correct behavior. The teachers reasoned that the correct behavior for Tina would be to keep her head still and to move it only upon instruction. So, the teacher sat behind Tina and gently held her head still for 15 seconds when she had a head-rolling episode. Then Tina was told to hold her head stationary in an upward direction for 15 seconds without movement. Five minutes of practice trials followed each head-rolling episode. Within one week, Tina rolled her head only half as much as she had before, demonstrating that the positive practice was effective, but that it did not totally stop the behavior.

Because the positive practice head restraint was partially effective, the teacher increased the number of practice trials, so that 20 minutes of practice were required instead of 5 minutes. Within four days of this longer practice duration, the head-rolling decreased to a near-zero level. On most days thereafter, the teacher no longer had to use the head restraint. Tina now participated in the class instruction, keeping her head stationary, thereby allowing her to attend closely to the teacher's instructions. She was later transferred to a higher level class, where she continued to refrain from headweaving.

Self-Test

1. In the above example, what was responsible for the eventual elimination of Tina's head-rolling?

   _____

   _____

2. Did the increased duration of practice give more opportunity for learning?
   Yes ☐   No ☐

3. Did the increased duration of practice involve more time and effort from Tina?   Yes ☐   No ☐

4. Did the positive practice work?   Yes ☐   No ☐

5. Do you think that Tina was annoyed by having to do the positive practice?
   Yes ☐   No ☐

6. Did the increased duration of practice help Tina to keep her head still?
   Yes ☐   No ☐

If your answer to the first question was "increased duration of practice," then your answer was correct. You should have answered "yes" to questions 2–6.

Occasional Versus Repeated Mistakes

If a mistake is made only occasionally, or if it is not a serious one, then a short duration of positive practice may be sufficient to prevent future mistakes. But for repeated mistakes, a longer duration of positive practice may be needed. For example, with Tina, a longer duration was needed because she had been rolling her head all day for years, and this action was hindering her school progress. Similarly, in the previous example of the child slamming the door, the action had occurred repeatedly. That was also true of Harold, who had repeatedly failed to catch the football. In all of these instances, the positive practice should have required many trials over many minutes in order to provide ample learning opportunities and more expenditure of time and effort.

On the other hand, if a child occasionally makes a mistake (such as forgetting once to brush his teeth or to wipe food from his chin) then one practice trial might be sufficient.

✏️ **Self-Test**

Based upon your own experiences, give two examples of a mistake that would require no more than one practice trial of positive practice.

Example 1: _____

_____

Example 2: _____

_____

Based upon your own experiences, give two examples of a mistake or misbehavior that would require many practice trials.

Example 1: _____

_____

_____

_____

Example 2: _____

_____

_____

_____

_____

Giving Positive Practice
Immediately After the Mistake

Positive practice should be performed as soon as possible after the mistake or misbehavior. By performing the practice immediately, the mistake or misbehavior is interrupted, and further mistakes or misbehaviors will not be practiced.

In an earlier example, a child's misbehavior in a special education class was reduced by having her raise her hand to ask permission to leave her seat. Initially, the teacher delayed the positive practice until the recess period. The result was a reduction of the misbehaviors from about 30 misbehaviors per day to only two per day. Then the teacher required at least one practice trial to be done immediately. The misbehaviors dropped to only one per day. Another advantage of giving the positive practice immediately is that the misbehavior is interrupted, thereby preventing a long episode of misbehavior.

Self-Test

Delaying the performance of positive practice:

1. Will make it less effective.   Yes ☐   No ☐
2. Will allow the mistakes to be repeated.   Yes ☐   No ☐
3. Will help the child realize why the practice was given.   Yes ☐   No ☐

The correct answers are (1) yes; (2) yes; and (3) no.

When Immediate Practice Is Inconvenient for the Parent

In some instances, great inconvenience would be caused to a parent or teacher if positive practice were given immediately after a mistake or misbehavior. The parent or teacher may be preoccupied, or the child's schedule may not allow time for practice.

One example of such an inconvenience would be a child who was misbehaving as he left the house to meet the school bus that was leaving very shortly. Another would be a teacher in a class of 30 students who saw a child bullying a smaller child while the teacher was busy giving the homework assignment right before the end of the class. Or the teacher of students with mental disabilities who saw one student picking his nose while she was taking a group of students from one building to another.

In the event that positive practice cannot be given immediately, give it as soon as convenient, just as the teacher did during the next recess period for the "hand raising practice" in the earlier example.

 Self-Test

When might positive practice be given in the following examples?

1. The boy who misbehaved just as he left his home to meet the school bus:

   _____

   _____

2. The teacher in the large class who observed one of her pupils bullying another as she was giving the homework assignment:

   _____

   _____

3. The teacher who observed a student picking his nose as she was guiding a group of students to another building:

   _____

   _____

In the above examples, the teacher or parent may not have had sufficient time to spend on extended positive practice, but if only one brief, immediate trial is possible, the misbehavior will be interrupted and the child will have experienced an immediate consequence. For example, the teacher of the student who was picking his nose could have had the child use a handkerchief to blow his nose, doing so only once. When the group reached the other building, the teacher could have required several practice trials.

How might a brief period of positive practice have been required immediately for:

(continues)

1. The teacher who observed the bullying incident right before the end of class?

_____

_____

2. The parent whose child misbehaved by throwing a piece of trash on the floor as he left for the school bus?

_____

_____

If you called for a very brief practice trial of the correct behavior, then your answers are correct.

Convenience for the Parent or Teacher

Because supervision of the child is required during positive practice, the parent or teacher should try to arrange the practice period at a convenient time. Yet, the requirement for immediacy, as we have seen, may result in the parent or teacher interrupting a class lecture, a guided walk, housework, a telephone conversation, or other activity.

Similarly, immediate practice may result in disruption of the child's necessary activities, such as catching the school bus, doing homework, doing work in class, or doing chores around the house.

Scheduling Positive Practice

The solution to this problem is to require only a brief practice trial immediately to interrupt or correct the misbehavior, and then to provide extended practice at a later time. The later time should be convenient to the parent or teacher and at a time when the child is not engaged in an essential activity.

Convenient times for a teacher to do the positive practice might be:

- Before school starts
- After school ends
- Recess period
- When the class is busy writing a report
- An independent project period

List other examples of convenient times for teachers.

Convenient times for a parent to supervise the positive practice might be:

- After dinner
- After the dinner plates have been put away
- Saturday morning or afternoon
- Sunday morning or afternoon
- After a telephone call has been completed
- After the housework is completed
- After the parent returns from work

List other examples of convenient time periods for parents.

The Child's Schedule

To select a time that would be least disruptive to the essential activities of a child, consider times when the child is engaged in leisure or recreation.

Periods for practice for a child might be when the child would otherwise be:

- Watching television
- Playing with toys

- Playing ball outside with other children
- Lying in bed and relaxing during the day
- "Doing nothing"

List other examples of periods that are least likely to be disruptive for your child, as well as most convenient for you.

_____

_____

_____

Giving Approval for the Correct Response

Giving Approval During Positive Practice

While the child is performing the positive practice trials, attention should be paid to the amount of approval given. If the parent or teacher gives abundant praise and snacks, the child may begin to misbehave in order to obtain the rewards that accompany the practice.

Example: Toilet Training

George learned how to toilet himself after his mother taught him with a positive practice training program. Whenever George wet his pants, the mother required him to perform 20 correct toileting trials, each trial consisting of the child rushing from a distant point in the home to the toilet and sitting momentarily on the toilet seat after lowering his pants. After each trial, the mother gave George a piece of cereal or a drink, praised him, and hugged him. After having been dry for several weeks after the initial training, George began wetting again. When the praise, snacks, and hugging were eliminated, the child stopped wetting. Apparently, the reinforcers had caused George to wet his pants deliberately to obtain the rewards.

Feedback and praise should not be eliminated entirely during positive practice because the child would then not know whether the practice was done correctly and also would not learn that the correct behavior would meet with approval.

The rule is to provide feedback and praise during the practice trials, but not to give excessive rewards. Tell the child in an enthusiastic manner that the practice is correct and give feedback about what should be improved if improvement is necessary.

The following example of positive practice in teaching correct eating illustrates how approval should be given.

Example: Proper Eating

A program for teaching proper eating had been completed in a ward of persons with profound and severe mental disabilities in an institution. The instructional program taught the students to raise their drinking glass with one hand rather than both hands; to keep the unused hand out of the food and on the lap; to use the knife, fork, or spoon rather than their hands; to use the proper utensil for each food; to put a new morsel of food in the mouth only after the previous morsel had been swallowed; to hold the utensil firmly enough to avoid spilling; to fill the spoon only partially to avoid spilling; to place the napkin on the lap; and to wipe the mouth and clothes if spilling occurred.

After training was completed, mistakes and accidents continued to occur for several students despite the fact that each student had learned how to perform each step correctly. To ensure that the students were motivated after training, the instructor walked around the table at each meal, warmly praising and patting the students in turn for correct eating behavior.

When a mistake occurred, however, the instructor required the student to practice the correct eating behavior. The instructor did so in a manner that provided feedback and praise.

When a student raised a glass of milk with both hands, for example, the instructor told the student disapprovingly that this was a mistake and required the student to lift the glass to his or her lips several times while guiding the student so that only one hand was used. The instructor gave a simple instruction to "Pick up the glass to your mouth," and then said, "Great, that's right," when the student finished doing so. Enthusiastic praise was given, but no other reward. At the end of each trial, the instructor said, "Now, pick up the glass to your mouth again." The instructor did not require or allow the student to drink from the glass at each trial, but only to bring the glass to the lips so that the correct use of one hand to raise the glass was practiced, but without the intake of milk. If allowed to drink, one might deliberately make errors in order to obtain the positive practice.

Similarly, if the mistake were overfilling the spoon (with spilling resulting), the instructor required several practice trials in which the student was guided in properly filling the spoon and bringing it to the lips. The instructor's comments were to "Pick up a little bit," "That's right," "You did that beautifully," and "Now, let's do it again," while patting the student's arm.

Self-Test

When food is spilled by a child because of overfilling the spoon, what should the instructor require as positive practice?

_____

_____

_____

1. Should the instructor point out that an error was made?   Yes ☐   No ☐

2. If the instructor, while going from one student to another, sees a student fill the spoon correctly as soon as a spill occurred, should the instructor give enthusiastic praise?   Yes ☐   No ☐

3. During positive practice should the instructor pat and praise the student as the student practices partially filling the spoon?   Yes ☐   No ☐

4. During positive practice should the instructor give an extra reward or snack for a correct response?   Yes ☐   No ☐

The correct answers are: (1) yes; (2) yes; (3) yes; and (4) no.

Giving Approval for Spontaneous Correct Behavior

The previous examples illustrate an important rule concerning the use of positive practice. Before positive practice is used, provide enthusiastic approval to the child for spontaneously engaging in the correct behavior.

For example, before requiring positive practice of a child who has not done his or her homework, the teacher or parent should have been showing enthusiastic approval on the occasions when the child did do the homework.

Self-Test: Stealing

Before requiring a child who steals objects to practice sharing and giving things to the victim, show approval when the child spontaneously

_____

_____

Self-Test: Cursing

Before a child who curses, insults, or criticizes his or her classmates is required to practice giving compliments and appreciation, the parent or teacher should give approval immediately after each time the child does positive things spontaneously.

Give examples of some very specific actions or statements for which the parent or teacher would watch and then give approval to the child, such as:

1. Offering to help

2. Compliments on clothing

3. Passing food at mealtime

4. Sharing a gift

5. _____

6. _____

7. _____

8. _____

9. _____

10. _____

When approval for spontaneous, correct behaviors is given, positive practice may be unnecessary for some children.

Example: Self-Stimulation

Positive practice was chosen as a means of eliminating self-stimulatory behavior in some institutionalized persons with severe mental disabilities. The behaviors included body rocking, headweaving, nose touching, and self-slapping. The intended positive practice consisted of requiring the persons to maintain head, body, hands, or fingers stationary for an extended period, moving that part of the body only when it was normal to do so, such as after an instruction.

Prior to initiating this positive practice for normal body movement, the instructor began to consistently reward students for normal body, hand, and head movements. The result was a reduction of these strange, repetitive, self-stimulatory behaviors for almost all students and a complete elimination for some of them. The high frequency of praise and rewards for the spontaneous correct behaviors reduced the need for a required period of practice trials.

Complete the following exercises by indicating examples of approval for correct behaviors accompanying positive practice.

Self-Test: Dirty Hands

A mother has been giving her child positive practice trials in washing his hands when she found them dirty at mealtime. Then he washes up on his own before one meal. What should the mother say and do at that time?

_____

_____

_____

Self-Test: Shouting

A teacher has been giving a student positive practice trials in speaking very softly whenever the student shouts in class. About one hour after a positive practice period, the teacher notices the child whispering to a classmate to avoid disturbing the class. What should the teacher say and do when she sees this?

_____

_____

_____

Manner of Explaining to the Child
the Positive Practice Rationale

Prior to initiating a positive practice program, the child should be given an explanation of what the correct response is, why it is desirable, and what the results should be. Manual guidance may be necessary for persons with severe mental disabilities because they are not likely to understand. An explanation or even a demonstration should be given to ensure that the children understand what is needed. This demonstration and explanation of the rationale will make the child more cooperative and more receptive to performing the positive practice, as well as less likely to object because of its abrupt imposition. The explanation is best given the day before the positive practice is to be used, so that ample time is allowed for the child to change his conduct spontaneously.

One method of increasing the cooperation of a young child is to explain the positive practice as a game, such as by calling it "The Show Me" game or "The Practice Makes Perfect" game. By demonstrating the practice game during the explanation, and by having the child perform a few practice trials before a mistake has been made, the child will be more inclined to cooperate when a mistake is actually made.

 Self-Test

How would you explain to a child the rationale for a positive practice procedure you intend to use for spelling mistakes?

_____

_____

_____

_____

_____

What If the Child Refuses To Do the Required Positive Practice?

If a child refuses to perform the positive practice, it is likely that the procedure is being used as a simple punishment. Positive practice differs from punishment. Yet, because of the effort and time that is required of the child to practice the positive aspect of the behavior, the child may feel it is punishment. To avoid the child's reaction to positive practice as a simple punishment, special attention should be paid to several important points relating to the differences between positive practice and punishment.

How Positive Practice Differs from Punishment

1. The child should be given an explanation of *why* the practice is needed at a time when the child and parent are in receptive and happy moods. This explanation should be given at least a day before the new rules are put into effect.

2. The use of positive practice for severe or continuous problem behaviors should be established as a *routine method* of dealing with problem misbehaviors. The child then becomes accustomed to this general strategy prior to initiating it for a new problem.

3. The parent should impose the positive practice requirement in a *calm, even-toned manner,* without anger, to avoid having the child view the requirement as a punishment.

4. The parent or teacher should demonstrate or explain the *specific details* of the correct response to be practiced in those instances where the child may not have learned how to perform it.

5. *Gentle manual guidance* should be used to assist the child as soon as the instruction is given, especially if the child is nonverbal, as with students who are mentally disabled. This manual guidance is a substitute for the verbal description of the correct response. Even if the child is verbal, the manual guidance will communicate the parent's resolution that the correct response must be practiced.

6. A child is likely to feel punished if he or she is told to "Go do your homework" or "You lose your allowance" when he or she misbehaves. But, the child should recognize that the parent's intent is to educate if he or she is required to practice proper behavior instead.

7. When the correct action is performed, give *feedback* about the correctness of the behavior and warmly praise the child whenever he or she performs the correct action spontaneously.

Positive practice is a method of eliminating the need for anger, punishment, criticism, nagging, and bad feelings. Instead, it emphasizes the positive and reasonable action that is needed to avoid problems now and in the future.

Self-Imposed Positive Practice

When a child deliberately misbehaves, the positive practice requirement must usually be imposed on an unwilling child. However, in dealing with older children or adults who are motivated to correct their problems, the practice can often be self-imposed. This self-imposition was seen in the example of the boy who practiced "getting-up" exercises on his own in order to prevent future bedwettings. Self-imposed positive practice can often be used by older children or adults when the problem behavior is caused by a deficiency of learning.

Self-Test: Stuttering

As part of a stuttering treatment program, a college student, Paul, was taught how to breathe smoothly. Paul had sought treatment because of the difficulties his stuttering caused in class discussions. The positive practice program consisted of having him breathe smoothly for about two minutes whenever he began to stutter. The instructor taught Paul how to breathe correctly and had him practice during an instructional session. Whenever Paul began to stutter in class, he stopped speaking momentarily and adopted the new breathing pattern for the next two minutes, and then continued his speaking, but in that breathing pattern. Within one week, the stuttering episodes had decreased to about 2% of the previous rate. After a month, Paul scarcely stuttered at all.

Was Paul motivated to eliminate his problem?

_____

_____

_____

What was the source of his motivation? _____

_____

_____

Was the duration of the positive practice specified?

_____

What was the duration? _____

Was the positive practice self-imposed? _____

_____

(continues)

By starting the smooth breathing as soon as Paul started to stutter, was that stuttering episode interrupted?

_____

_____

_____

The correct answers are that Paul was strongly motivated to eliminate the stuttering because of the interference with his college progress, and so the practice was self-imposed. The stuttering episode was interrupted immediately and the positive practice was engaged in for the specified two minutes.

Self-Test: A Head Jerking Tic

Mrs. Trapelo, a housewife, was very embarrassed by her nervous habit of jerking her head to the side. She obtained instruction on how to control it by tensing her neck muscles.

How would you instruct Mrs. Trapelo in the use of a positive practice program for eliminating this head-jerking tic? Specifically:

What would you designate as the correct response to be practiced?

_____

When should she perform this correct response?

_____

For how long? _____

Would this be an example of self-imposed positive practice?

_____

The correct answers are that Mrs. Trapelo would be instructed to tense her neck muscles for about two minutes as soon as her head started to move.

This practice would have to be self-imposed because she is an adult. Her motivation to eliminate this habit is so great that she should have no trouble following the instructions.

Can you describe a similar application of positive practice from your own experience?

_____

_____

_____

_____

_____

_____

_____

_____

Keeping a Record

Keeping a record of the behavior being treated helps in evaluating the effectiveness of positive practice. Keeping a record also provides a clear basis for discussion with and feedback from a supervisor.

The record should be started several days before positive practice is begun in order to provide a measure of the pre-training behavior of the child. At least one week of pre-training record-keeping is advisable.

Below is a sample record for a child who was mistreating his younger sister. The positive practice procedure required him to reassure, help, and praise his sister.

Sample Record

Date	No. of Misbehaviors		Comments
Jan. 4	⊞ II	7	I scolded him after each fight.
Jan. 5	II	2	His father spanked him after one bad incident.
Jan. 6	III	3	I tried ignoring it, but couldn't.
Jan. 7	⊞	5	Still tried to ignore, finally sent him to his room.
Jan. 8	II	2	His sister was with friends visiting most of the day.
Jan. 9	⊞ I	6	I was too busy to break up the fights; yelled at him.
Jan. 10	III	3	Explained positive practice procedure in morning.

Started Positive Practice

Date	No. of Misbehaviors		Comments
Jan. 11	II	2	He didn't mind the practice, but he did mind missing the TV show the first time. The second time he insisted it wasn't his fault, but still practiced when I insisted.
Jan. 12	I	1	He cooperated in the practice, but didn't like it. He helped his sister an hour later with her flute. I praised him and gave both ice cream.
Jan. 13		0	Didn't tease or hit; ignored his sister.
Jan. 14		0	They went to store together and did not fight. I told him I was proud (and his father told him that, too) and offered to take both to the movies.
Jan. 15		0	Getting along fine. Watched TV together.
Jan. 16		0	Had sister play with his friend; gave all French fries.
Jan. 17		0	Sister helped prepare for his birthday.
Jan. 18	I	1	Had one fight. I gave only brief (1-minute) practice since this looked like an accident.
Jan. 19		0	Still playing together and no fights.
Jan. 20		0	I bought them a checker set for getting along so well.

The record includes a separate line for each date to be written in the left column. Each day should be noted even if no misbehavior occurred on that day. A tally mark is put in the second column for each misbehavior and the total for each day is entered in the third column. The last column is for comments to be used when discussing the progress with a counselor and to ascertain what one is doing. The triple horizontal lines indicate when positive practice was initiated (Jan. 11) and the positive practice program began.

Exercise in Using Positive Practice

Use of Positive Practice by Others

Describe a situation from your experience in which someone used positive practice.

_____

_____

_____

_____

_____

_____

Describe a situation from your experience in which positive practice should have been used.

_____

_____

_____

_____

_____

_____

(continues)

Of the children for which you care, describe how you might use positive practice for their problems.

1. Name of child: _____

   Describe the nature of the problem behavior.

   _____

   _____

   _____

   _____

   Identify the correct behavior. _____

   _____

   _____

   _____

   What would be the positive practice requirement?

   _____

   _____

   _____

2. Name of child: _____

   Describe the nature of the problem behavior.

   _____

   _____

   _____

   _____

(continues)

Identify the correct behavior. _____

_____

_____

_____

What would be the positive practice requirement?

_____

_____

_____

Use with One's Own Children

In the space below, describe how you will use positive practice for a problem behavior of your own child.

Name of child: _____

Problem behavior exhibited: _____

_____

Correct behavior to be used: _____

_____

Number of trials to be given: _____

Number of minutes to be given: _____

(continues)

When will the positive practice program be initiated?

_____

How much time will there be between the explanation of the positive practice and its initiation?

_____

Time of explanation: _____

Place of explanation: _____

Will the correct response be rewarded when it occurs spontaneously?
   Yes ☐   No ☐

How will you reward it? _____

_____

When (what date) will you start looking for and reacting to the spontaneous correct responses?

_____

Will rewards and praise be given for the correct responses made during the series of positive practice trials?   Yes ☐   No ☐

Will feedback be given?   Yes ☐   No ☐

What specifically will you say? _____

_____

_____

If it is inconvenient to give the series of positive practice trials at the moment of the misbehavior, will you give at least one trial then?   Yes ☐   No ☐

What later, more convenient time period will you use to give the rest of the practice trials?

_____

_____

(continues)

Prepare a recording sheet and start to record the misbehaviors. Write the information in the space below, or on any sheet of lined paper.

Recording Form

Date	Number of Misbehaviors	Comments

Describe the results of your use of positive practice.

Did the misbehavior decrease? _____

Did the child show annoyance at being required to do the practice?

_____

Did the child perform the positive practice correctly?

_____

Did the child perform the correct response spontaneously at any time?

_____

Describe. _____

_____

_____

What changes would you make in your training procedure the next time that you use positive practice?

_____

_____

_____

(continues)

Describe any other noteworthy aspects of the procedure or of your child's behavior.

_____

_____

_____

_____

Part II. The Principle of Self-Correction and Overcorrection

Introduction to Self-Correction and Overcorrection

Taking Responsibility for One's Actions

The underlying principle of self-correction and overcorrection is that *we should take responsibility for our own actions when we cause annoyance or disruption to others.* By correcting the situation, we eliminate the annoyance. By overcorrection, rather than simple correction, we demonstrate to the annoyed person that we care greatly that he or she was inconvenienced and that we wish to "make up" for our inappropriate action.

Too Much Help

One major cause of irresponsible conduct by a child is the desire of the parent to help the child. An infant must have help. As the infant matures, however, the parent can easily form the habit of providing so much help that the child does not learn to take responsibility for his or her own actions. Self-correction and overcorrection restore this responsibility.

When Criticism Does Not Work

Another cause of careless conduct is our tendency to react to carelessness by giving criticism or by awarding a bad grade in school, neither of which may be of great concern to some persons. Self-correction and overcorrection, however, require time and effort from the careless person, thereby encouraging that person to be more careful. The greater the time and effort required in self-correcting, the greater will be the interest of the person to be more careful in the future—which is why overcorrection is more effective than simple correction.

Long-Term Benefit of Using Overcorrection

Ironically, this same time factor may be the cause of careless conduct by children. When a child leaves a toy outside, for example, the mother may feel that it takes less time for her to put the toy in its proper place than to require the child to do so. The time-saving may be real for one such incident, but, in the long term, the mother will have saved herself far more time if the child learns to be responsible and to self-correct.

Because the mother puts the toys away, the child has no incentive to do so himself and may become more and more careless until the mother becomes angry. By spending a few minutes requiring self-correction in the beginning, the mother makes a wise investment that may save many hours in the future.

Reacting Constructively Rather Than with Guilt or Anger

When a child takes another person's property or breaks someone else's possession, criticism and punishment may create a guilty feeling, but the stolen or broken property is not restored. Self-correction on the other hand requires the child to either return the item or its equivalent, or to repair the damaged item. The owner of the property no longer needs to feel angry and inclined to punish the child. The child, in turn, need not be made to feel guilty.

Self-correction and overcorrection provide a constructive replacement for punishment and guilt.

Examples of Self-Correction and Overcorrection

Self-Correction and Overcorrection with Young Children

Fred was an active 4-year-old who often forgot to take care of his belongings. Most annoying was his habit of leaving a trail of debris when he entered the house. He would leave the door open, throw his coat on the sofa, kick his sneakers off on the living room floor, and leave his baseball and bat in the hall—all despite constant reminders, threats, and punishments. His mother spent so much time picking up after him that she had less time for her other activities and thus became very annoyed with Fred.

She and her husband decided to use self-correction and overcorrection. They told Fred that they would stop picking up after him and that, in the future, he would be required to interrupt whatever he was doing to go back, pick up everything, and put it in its place each time he left something out. In addition, he would overcorrect by putting away anything else in the room that was out of place, to the satisfaction of the annoyed person. After explaining and discussing the plan in detail, they role-played a typical scene so that Fred clearly understood the new rules.

The next two days Fred was very neat, but the third day he was in a rush to watch a TV show and again left the door open and his clothes and toys scattered all about the hallway. His mother interrupted the TV viewing and directed him to close the door and put each of his things in its proper place. She then required him to straighten out the living room and arrange the sofa cushions. She avoided threats or criticism. Because Fred cleaned up very slowly, he missed all but five minutes of the TV show that he had wanted to see. The next day he again forgot to close the door, but he corrected it before his mother noticed. From then on, he rarely needed a reminder, but, when he did, he quickly cleaned up and then called his mother to inspect his work.

Self-Correction and Overcorrection at School

Joan was a fourth grader who was receiving bad grades because of her failure to do her homework on time. After two months of consistently late homework, Joan's teacher told her that when future assignments were not completed, she would spend her recess in class. If necessary, Joan would have to stay 15 minutes after school to complete the assignment. As overcorrection, an extra assignment would be given on that same topic. The teacher discussed with Joan the details of the rules and answered all her questions. They continued the discussion until Joan agreed that the new rule was reasonable and fair and that she would follow it. To assure Joan's understanding of the new rule, the teacher asked Joan questions about the details of the arrangement.

After two days of missing recesses and staying late after school, Joan began handing in her homework on time. The teacher was assisted by Joan's mother (who had been informed and approved of the program). The mother used overcorrection at home by having Joan start her homework right after eating supper rather than just prior to bedtime.

Self-Correction and Overcorrection with One's Spouse

Mrs. Blackburn dreaded going to parties with her husband because he often left her alone while he conversed with friends. They had frequent arguments because of his neglect. She suggested a self-correction and overcorrection strategy in which he would come to her side upon a prearranged signal from her. He would self-correct by remaining with her for at least 10 minutes or until she was comfortable talking to someone else. As overcorrection, Mr. Blackburn suggested that in addition he would introduce her to any friends with whom he began conversing and would involve her in the conversations by asking her opinion. They discussed the details of the arrangement until they agreed it was reasonable and fair to both of them. Mrs. Blackburn no longer felt uncomfortable at the parties, and the arguments about being ignored stopped. At a later date, Mr. Blackburn suggested that she follow the same correction procedure when he found himself uncomfortable and alone at parties with her friends.

The incidents and examples above illustrate how self-correction and overcorrection procedures not only decrease undesired behaviors, but also improve the disturbed situations caused by the behaviors. We turn now to a more detailed analysis of the general concept of overcorrection and the manner in which it is applied to different problems.

Defining Overcorrection

Overcorrection can be described in several ways:

- It is making a situation better than it was before the error or annoyance occurred.
- It is undoing a disturbed situation and improving it so that it is better than it was before the disturbance.
- It is "making things up to someone" by extra effort.
- It is a way of showing by immediate actions that one did not mean to inconvenience or hurt someone else.

In your own words, write what *overcorrection* is and what it accomplishes.

What it is: _____

_____

_____

What it accomplishes: _____

_____

_____

Describe a situation from your experience in which someone practiced overcorrection:

_____

_____

Describe a situation from your experience in which overcorrection should have been used but was not.

_____

_____

_____

_____

_____

The Correction Should Suit the Offense

In using overcorrection, the nature of the mistake should determine the nature of the overcorrection; otherwise the correction is only punishment. If a child is spanked, criticized, grounded, or has privileges removed, the penalties only punish the child for what he did wrong and do not teach the child what is correct. Check the answers below to indicate whether the action is an overcorrection or a punishment.

A child stays up an hour past his bedtime. The parent reacts by:

1. Criticizing him for being disobedient.
   Punishment ☐   Overcorrection ☐

2. Not allowing him to go to a movie the next day.
   Punishment ☐   Overcorrection ☐

3. Making him go to bed an hour and a half earlier the next night.
   Punishment ☐   Overcorrection ☐

4. Spanking him.
   Punishment ☐   Overcorrection ☐

If you checked overcorrection for number 3, you have the correct answer. The answer to numbers 1, 2, and 4 is punishment.

The following are some examples of overcorrection:

Problem	Examples of Self-Correction or Overcorrection
1. A child spills food from her overfilled spoon while eating very rapidly.	1. a) The child cleans up the spill. b) The child eats the rest of the meal very slowly, with the spoon only 1/4 filled.
2. A child loses an item that he borrowed.	2. a) The child is required to spend one hour looking for the item. b) The child offers, and gives, some other item of value to the person from whom it was borrowed.

(continues)

Problem	Examples of Self-Correction or Overcorrection
3. A driver of a car exceeds the speed limit.	3. The driver must take, and pay for, a driver's license test or go to driver's school.
4. Parent learns that her child stole and item from a store.	4. Child returns the item and pays the store an additional amount from his allowance.
5. A child is being a bully in school.	5. The teacher requires the bully to do something nice for five students each day for a week and to report it to the teacher.
6. A child calls his sister a bad name.	6. a) The mother has him give his sister compliments about how nice she looks and acts. b) The mother has him apologize to his sister and say nice things about her until the sister is no longer upset.

Exercises in Using Self-Correction and Overcorrection

Select and perform one or more of the following exercises:

Exercise 1: Self-Correction and Overcorrection When a Child Spills Something

Every young child occasionally spills or drops an object such as a glass of milk, a box of cereal, or something else that dirties the floor. If the child is very young, the parent usually cleans it up. When this happens with your child, proceed as follows:

1. Before the spill occurs, explain to the child that whenever something spills, he or she must clean it up.

2. Role-play an accident in which you drop something and then immediately clean it up, describing your actions as you do so.

3. Have the child pretend that he or she dropped something by mistake and have him or her clean it up, guiding his or her hands if necessary.

4. The next time the child spills something, wait about five seconds to see if he or she will start cleaning up without a reminder.

5. If the child does not start cleaning up, remind him or her to do so. Do not criticize or become angry.

(continues)

6. If the cleaning is very difficult, offer to help ("Here, I'll show you how") by manually guiding the child's hands, but do not do it for him or her. Have the child do at least part of the cleaning.

7. Praise the child for completing the cleanup.

8. Similarly, have the child straighten up any other items in the room. This aspect constitutes the overcorrection.

9. Compliment the child for correcting the situation.

Write what happened: _____

_____

_____

_____

Did you feel angry when the spill occurred?
Yes ☐   No ☐

Did you feel angry after the spill was cleaned up?
Yes ☐   No ☐

Did you feel that it would have been easier to clean the spill yourself?
Yes ☐   No ☐

As the child was cleaning up, did you feel tempted to do it yourself?
Yes ☐   No ☐

Did the child seem relieved that he or she would not be scolded or punished?
Yes ☐   No ☐

Did the child say anything that suggested he or she would be more careful in the future?
Yes ☐   No ☐

If so, what did the child say? _____

If not, what would you guess about his or her future behavior?

_____

As stated earlier, overcorrection is designed to substitute a constructive reaction to misbehavior for the more usual reaction of punishment. By reacting in this positive manner, our emotional reaction is also likely to be changed from anger to satisfaction that the problem has been remedied. Similarly, the offender's emotional reaction should change from a feeling of guilt to a feeling of relief.

Exercise 2: Self-Imposed Overcorrection When You Yourself Have Unintentionally Offended Someone

Think of someone you love and whom you do not wish to offend. The next time you annoy that person because of something you said, or did, or forgot to do, offer to overcorrect. You should select a type of correction you can perform immediately.

Write what happened: _____

_____

_____

_____

Did the person remain angry when you offered to overcorrect?
Yes ☐   No ☐

Did the person remain angry while you were overcorrecting?
Yes ☐   No ☐

After you finished overcorrecting, did you still feel annoyed at yourself?
Yes ☐   No ☐

Did the person refuse your offer to overcorrect at first?
Yes ☐   No ☐

If so, did you overcorrect in spite of his or her refusal?
Yes ☐   No ☐

Did you initially try to defend the action that caused annoyance?
Yes ☐   No ☐

Did you start the overcorrection immediately?
Yes ☐   No ☐

Exercise 3: Suggesting Correction and Overcorrection for Happenings in the Community or Nation

Newspapers usually contain stories of crimes or incidents where people hurt or annoy someone else. Select three examples from a current newspaper in which overcorrection could have been used. For each example, describe (a) what the

(continues)

incident was, (b) what penalty occurred or probably will occur, (c) what type of simple correction could be used for that incident, and (d) what type of over-correction could be used.

Newspaper Incident #1

a. Describe the incident or crime. _____

_____

_____

b. What penalty occurred or probably will occur?

_____

_____

_____

c. What type of simple self-correction could be used for the incident?

_____

_____

_____

d. What type of overcorrection could be used?

_____

_____

_____

Newspaper Incident #2

a. Describe the incident or crime. _____

_____

_____

(continues)

b. What penalty occurred or probably will occur?

_____

_____

_____

_____

c. What type of simple self-correction could be used for the incident?

_____

_____

_____

_____

d. What type of overcorrection could be used?

_____

_____

_____

Newspaper Incident #3

a. Describe the incident or crime. _____

_____

_____

_____

b. What penalty occurred or probably will occur?

_____

_____

_____

(continues)

c. What type of simple self-correction could be used for the incident?

_____

_____

_____

d. What type of overcorrection could be used?

_____

_____

_____

Simple Correction Versus Overcorrection

Simple correction means that the problem situation is corrected. Overcorrection means that not only was simple correction provided, but also the situation was improved until it was better than it had been prior to the problem. For example, if you accidentally broke a vase at a party, you would be practicing simple correction if you replaced it with an identical vase. If you desired to overcorrect, you would buy the host a vase that was even better than the one you broke.

In the following sample situations, describe what actions constitute simple self-correction and what actions are overcorrection.

A woman on a diet has promised herself not to eat dessert for a week. She has been successful for five days, but, on the sixth day, she eats a slice of cheesecake that adds 100 calories to what she had set as a maximum for the day.

Possible simple self-correction: _____

_____

_____

(continues)

Possible overcorrection: _____

_____

_____

_____

You have the right idea if you said that for simple self-correction, she should eat 100 calories less than her diet calls for the following day, and for overcorrection, she should eat more than 100 calories less the next day or perhaps 100 calories less for the next two days.

A child had been asked to stop at the grocery store for some milk on his way home from school, but he arrives home without it. His mother needs the milk for a special recipe.

Possible simple self-correction: _____

_____

_____

Possible overcorrection: _____

_____

_____

If you said a simple self-correction would be for him to go back out for the milk, you are right. An overcorrection would be to go for the milk and then do some other tasks to help his mother, such as set the table, vacuum the dining room rug, or do the dishes. He also might obtain additional needed items at the same store or another store.

A child awakens 15 minutes past the scheduled wake-up time. As a result, she is 15 minutes late for school that day. The parent decides to use a correction procedure.

Possible simple self-correction: _____

_____

_____

Possible overcorrection: _____

_____

_____

One simple correction procedure the parent might use would be to require the child to awaken 15 minutes earlier the next day. An overcorrection procedure might be to have the child awaken 30 minutes earlier the following day(s) or go to bed earlier in the evening.

Simple correction is usually sufficient when the problem is not severe, or when the problem has not occurred repeatedly, when the action was accidental rather than deliberate, or when the action does not severely annoy the other person. But, if the problem is major, repeated, deliberate, or causes severe annoyance, then overcorrection should be used to give assurance to the victim that the problem will not be repeated. For example, if a child leaves his clothes lying about the living room after repeated reminders from his mother, the persistence of this habit suggests that simple correction might be ineffective. Simple correction might consist of having him interrupt his activities to pick up the clothes. For overcorrection, he might be required to pick up other items in the living room.

In each of the following situations, describe whether simple correction or overcorrection should be used. Give a reason for your decision and suggest what type of correction or overcorrection you might use to solve the problem.

A child deliberately struck another child and made his nose bleed. The teacher concluded after questioning the children that the action was entirely unjustified and decided to require the aggressive child to correct the situation. The problem, as the teacher viewed it, was that the physical injury had to be cared for and that the victim was very upset.

(continues)

Preferred Solution: Simple Self-Correction _____? or Overcorrection _____?

State the reason for your decision. _____

_____

_____

What types of actions might you require for the simple self-correction?

_____

_____

_____

_____

You are correct if you suggest overcorrection since the child's action was deliberate. The aggressive child might be required to help treat the nose-bleed, reassure the victim, and give the victim something special.

A child fails to turn off the light as she leaves her room. The parents had established the rule that lights should always be turned off when not in use in order to conserve energy. The child had always followed this rule in the past but was in a rush this time and seemed to have forgotten.

Preferred Solution: Simple Self-Correction _____? or Overcorrection _____?

State the reason for your choice. _____

_____

What actions might you require for the simple self-correction?

_____

_____

_____

(continues)

If the problem were habitual and required overcorrection, what might you do?

_____

_____

_____

If you suggested having the child check that all unnecessary lights were turned off in all the rooms in the house, that would be correct.

A wife is heartbroken that her husband has forgotten their anniversary. Usually he buys her clothing or jewelry valued at $50–$100. When she reminds him of the anniversary that evening, he is filled with regret and begins thinking of excuses to justify his forgetfulness. But, instead, he decides to correct the situation.

Preferred Solution: Simple Self-Correction _____? or Overcorrection _____?

State the reason for your choice. _____

_____

_____

What action(s) might he take for the simple self-correction?

_____

_____

_____

What action(s) might he take for overcorrection? _____

_____

_____

Would the correction he suggested be more effective if it were performed that evening or the next day?

_____

Because his wife was very disappointed, the preferred solution would be to overcorrect by giving her a gift that was more expensive than usual that same evening, if possible.

A child repeatedly cuts in front of other children standing in line at the school cafeteria. The teacher decides that the correction requirement will be for the child to go to the end of the line. The teacher discusses it with the child before-hand to make him aware of the new rule.

Preferred Solution: Simple Self-Correction _____? or Overcorrection _____?

State the reason for your choice. _____

_____

_____

What type of action might the teacher specify for simple self-correction?

_____

_____

_____

What type of action might the teacher specify for overcorrection?

_____

_____

The correct answer is that overcorrection would be preferable, because the action has occurred repeatedly, it was deliberate, and it caused extreme annoyance.

Simple correction might be to go to the end of the line. Overcorrection might be to have him wait until all of the others have been served.

A complaint has been made to a waiter by a couple in a restaurant because they waited for 40 minutes after placing their order for dinner. The problem is that they ordered an item on the menu that required lengthy preparation, but they were not told of this delay when they ordered. Also, the waiter forgot to bring the medium-priced appetizer they had ordered. Since the restaurant had only recently opened for business, the owner was eager to have good public relations.

Preferred Solution: Simple Self-Correction _____? or Overcorrection _____?

State the reason(s) for your decision. _____

_____

_____

_____

What would be a simple correction the waiter could perform?

_____

_____

_____

What might be an overcorrection the waiter could perform?

_____

_____

_____

_____

Since the problem was serious, the manager would use both simple self-correction and overcorrection. A simple correction would be to bring the appetizer immediately and ask the chef to hurry preparation of the main course. An overcorrection would be possibly to offer an extra item that would be brought immediately and without charge, such as an extra appetizer, drink, or salad as well as a complimentary dessert.

What If the Situation Cannot Be Corrected?

Not all situations permit complete correction; the disturbance is irreversible. For example, if a child breaks a windowpane, the glass cannot be put back together. If milk is spilled on the floor, the milk cannot be returned to the glass or container. If money is stolen by a child, it cannot be returned if it were spent and the child has no other income.

Another reason why correction may not be possible is that the magnitude of the correction, even simple correction, is beyond the resources of the person. For example, a group of young children set a fire in a schoolroom at night causing thousands of dollars of damage. Or a man with mental disabilities in an institution breaks a chair in a temper tantrum. Or a woman who is mentally ill in a state hospital tears her clothing to shreds. It is impossible for anyone to make the clothing intact, to restore the chair fully, or to restore the original classroom. In addition, the young child, the institutionalized man, and the mentally ill woman do not have the money or skill to complete a major correction, even if it were possible.

When correction is not possible because the disturbance is irreversible or beyond the person's means, the general rule to follow is to have the person provide as much of the correction as possible.

The important consideration is that the person spend sufficient time and effort to realize that he or she must take responsibility for the actions. Only in that way can the person experience the inconvenience suffered by the other person(s) who must correct the disturbance and thus become aware of the consequences of his or her action.

Requiring Effort for a Partial Correction

The rule in requiring time and effort suggests that the child who spilled the milk on the floor should clean up the floor, even if the milk cannot be returned to the glass. The child who broke the pane of glass should clean up the pieces, even if the damage is permanent. He or she could, of course, be required to phone or visit the necessary stores to obtain a new pane, to measure the window, to obtain the ruler for measurement, and to be present while the glass is installed, assisting at every step, even if the child cannot install it because of the lack of skill.

A general rule to follow when requiring correction is to require the person *(1) to be present at all points in the correction* and *(2) to assist with any part of the correction that he or she is able to perform*. His or her presence and assistance may not be of great value to the person who must correct the situation, but it will teach the person who caused the problem that time and effort are required and that correction is the responsibility of the person who caused the problem.

In the case where a financial loss is too great for the person to repay, the principle suggests that payment be made to the fullest extent possible.

One method of achieving adequate repayment is for the payments to be spread over a long time. For example, each of the boys who caused the thousands of dollars damage by setting fire to the classroom might be required to pay one or two dollars a week from his allowance every week for two or three years. If he has no money whatsoever, he might be required to work each week to pay for his offense by helping the janitor clean up all inflammable materials and by checking all doors and windows at closing time to ensure they are locked against other vandals. Because *the corrective action should be related to the offense,* this work should be done at the school, which was the scene of the fire. If that is not possible, then the work may be done elsewhere. The parents might require a few hours of non-paid work at home each week for a child who is bussed to school and cannot spend extra time in school.

 Self-Test

A 4-year-old child deliberately breaks her sister's piggy bank, resulting in glass being scattered on the rug. She is too young to be trusted to pick up the glass. The father scolds her and sends her to her room while he cleans up the damage. He obtains a trash can from the kitchen, a vacuum cleaner from the closet, an extension cord from the garage, work gloves from his work bench, and cleans up all the glass. He then empties the trash can and returns each of the items to its correct place. He then talks to the girl's sister, reassures her, and goes to the store to buy a replacement. During this time, the child who broke the piggy bank is in her room playing with one of her own toys.

The mother has observed all of these activities and decided that a correction strategy would have been preferable. But, the father tells her that their daughter is too young to correct the damage, that the glass is too dangerous, and that the child does not have the money to replace her sister's bank.

In the following spaces, state what the mother might suggest to the father for future incidents of this nature.

(continues)

What should the child be required to do in cleaning up?

_____

_____

_____

_____

What should the child be required to do in obtaining a replacement?

_____

_____

_____

_____

What might the child be required to do to reassure her sister?

_____

_____

_____

The correction procedure should have required the child to perform as many of the activities as possible that the father had performed. The child should have been accompanied by the father while she obtained the extension cord after he directed her to its proper location. The father might have assisted her in lifting the vacuum cleaner out of the closet, but have had the child pull it to the scene of the accident. The child could probably obtain and carry the trash container as well as the gloves with no assistance from the father. While the father alone should pick up the larger pieces of broken glass, the child should be present rather than in her room. To reassure the child's sister, the father might have had the child apologize, shake hands with her, obtain a handkerchief for her tears, stroke her shoulder, and offer her own toys as replacements for the broken bank.

If purchase of a replacement were necessary, the young child should have accompanied the father to the store, looked for possible replacements in the store, and carried the item purchased. Because the child probably has little allowance at her age, she might not have been able to pay for the purchased replacement. But, if she did have an allowance of 5 cents a week, she might have been required to pay 2 cents each week for 10 weeks, even though this would amount to only 20 cents and the replacement cost might be $2. She could have reassured her sister until her sister was no longer upset, and she could have given her sister the replacement toy herself.

How To Decide on the Type of Correction

Some useful rules can be followed to help in specifying the nature of the overcorrection.

We previously presented one rule for determining whether or not to use overcorrection. *Overcorrection is best when the problem is deliberate, frequent, severe, or very annoying.*

A second rule is to ask, *What are the actions needed to restore the situation to the state that existed before the problem?* This question is often answered by listing all the specific actions you would have to perform if you personally corrected the situation. In the case of a person who broke an item of value to you, it would be insufficient to simply have the person pay you the cost of a replacement. You would still be required to go to the department store, search for the replacement, and pay for it. Consequently, even simple self-correction means that all of these actions should be required.

A third rule to follow in deciding on the type of correction is to ask, *What would you yourself do as a socially sensitive person if you had accidentally created the problem.* For example, in deciding on a suitable correction for a child who cuts into a line of waiting people, ask yourself what you would do if you had inadvertently cut into line. Most likely you would apologize and go to the end of the line. This is also the type of simple self-correction you could require of a student or child.

 Self-Test

Jim is a teenager who obtained his driver's license only two months ago. He scraped the paint on the family car while backing out of the garage to go out on a date. The cost of repainting the car at the body shop was $300, but Jim earned only $10 a week on his part-time job and needed most of it for expenses his parents considered important.

Possible correction solution: Describe in very specific detail the actions Jim's parents might require of him to correct the damage to the car, at least partially, if Jim is to attempt it himself.

(continues)

Describe the corrective action that might be required of Jim if he is to have a body shop do the repair.

What If the Person Refuses To Perform the Self-Correction or Overcorrection?

Self-correction requires a person to take responsibility for his or her disruptive actions to avoid the anger of other persons who are inconvenienced by the disruption. If a child refuses to perform a suggested overcorrection, the alternative is for him or her to face a different penalty that may include the loss of privileges or some other disciplinary action that is far less desirable to the child than self-correction.

A rule to follow in the case of a refusal to self-correct is *to remind the child what the more severe disciplinary action will be and, if the refusal persists, then impose that discipline.*

The second rule to follow to prevent refusal to self-correct is *to discuss the need for self-correction before the incident occurs.* Otherwise, the child or the adult may become quite emotional at the moment of the disruption and find it difficult to engage in constructive self-correction with the child if the disruption is something that has occurred several times in the past. This is the same as was described for positive practice previously.

A third rule is *to establish self-correction as a habit for any disruption.* The child will then be accustomed to self-correcting and will be less likely to refuse when a new situation arises.

For very young children, a useful rule is *to guide the child manually and gently through the corrective action if the child refuses or delays to self-correct.* This rule requires that the parent give the instruction to self-correct only when standing next to the child so that the manual guidance can be given one or two seconds after the instruction. With respect to adults, the decision to self-correct must be made voluntarily by the adult and thus cannot be required by someone else in the event of a refusal. But, self-correction is such a reasonable and pleasant solution to problems that adults are usually willing to self-correct, rather than becoming defensive, especially if the guideline above had been discussed previously.

 Self-Test

A 5-year-old boy frequently fails to change into his play clothes and instead plays in his "new" clothes, causing them to become prematurely dirty or torn. In the past, the parents have become very upset and punished the child by not permitting him to play outside for several days.

The parents decide to use simple self-correction by requiring the child to change himself into clean play clothes, and then to wash the dirtied new clothes, fold them, and put them away. As overcorrection, since this problem is repetitive, the parents also intend to require him to wash and put away the other clothes in the laundry hamper. The parents expect the child to refuse when they tell him to do these corrections the next time he comes home with dirtied new clothes.

One of the rules for preventing refusals is to discuss and role-play the self-correction beforehand. What should the parents tell the child in this discussion?

_____

_____

_____

_____

_____

A second rule for refusals is to make self-correction a habit. What other common misbehaviors might the parents deal with through self-correction?

_____

_____

_____

_____

_____

(continues)

A third rule for refusals is to notify the person of the alternative form of discipline for the misbehavior. What is the alternative in this case?

_____

_____

_____

_____

_____

Gentle manual guidance is the fourth rule for dealing with refusals. How could the parents apply this rule to this child?

_____

_____

_____

_____

_____

_____

Self-Correction Differs from Punishment

The guiding principle in self-correction is that the self-correction, like positive practice, is different from simple punishment. Yet, a feeling of punishment may exist in the child because of the effort he or she must make to self-correct. The mother of the child may also behave as if she were giving punishment because the episode has caused her to be annoyed. To avoid the feeling of punishment, several precautions can be taken similar to those taken with positive practice.

1. The parents _should not speak in an angry, loud, or critical voice._ They should speak calmly, softly, and sympathetically.

2. As noted previously, _the child must have agreed beforehand to the reasonableness of the self-correction_ when the parents and child discussed it

together. In this discussion, the parents should adopt the spirit of compromise in order to obtain agreement and cooperation. For example, if a child objects strongly to a proposed rule that 60 minutes of extra study be required for a poor grade at school, the parents should consider a compromise of 30 minutes, if that duration will gain the child's cooperation. If the problem persists, then the duration might be increased at that time.

3. The parents *should express themselves in positive terms.* Avoid using negative terms that state what the child should not do, such as, "Don't clutter up the house," "Don't be late," "Don't hit your sister," "Stop shouting," or "Don't write so sloppily." Instead, use positive expressions to tell the child what actions are needed, such as, "Pick up your clothes," "Be home by five o'clock," "Help your sister with the dishes," "Speak more softly while I'm on the phone," or "Leave a one-inch margin on the paper."

Self-correction is a positive approach that eliminates the need for anger, punishment, criticisms, or nagging, and instead emphasizes what positive and reasonable action is needed. By following the preceding guidelines, you can avoid the feeling that self-correction is punishment.

Keeping a Record

Purpose of Records

Most studies of overcorrection show a substantial decrease of the problem behavior within two or three days. The effect of overcorrection is seen more vividly if a daily record of the behavior is kept. The daily record can include comments about the procedure and the behavior that are helpful in discussing the progress with a counselor or instructor. Below is a sample of a record for a child who left his toys lying about the house. This method of recording is similar to the method described previously for positive practice.

Sample Record

Date	No. of Misbehaviors		Comments
Oct. 22	⊪⊦	5	I picked up the toys each time for him.
Oct. 23	|||	3	I picked up the toys each time for him.
Oct. 24	||||	4	I picked up the toys each time for him.
Oct. 25	⊪⊦|	6	I picked up the toys each time for him.
Oct. 26	||	2	He picked up toys and put them in his room. Complained the first time.

(continues)

Date	No. of Misbehaviors		Comments
Oct. 27		0	His father also talked to him about overcorrection. Praised for neatness.
Oct. 28	I	1	No compaints by him. Still played with toys but put them away.
Oct. 29		0	Told him I was proud.
Oct. 30		0	Told him I was proud.
Oct. 31		0	Told him I was proud.
Nov. 1		0	Told him I was proud.
Nov. 2		0	Told him I was proud.

The record includes a separate line for each date to be written in the left column. Each day should be noted even if no misbehavior occurred on that date. A tally mark is put in the second column for each misbehavior, and the total for each day is entered in the third column. The fourth column is for comments the parent may use when discussing the progress with the counselor or instructor. The triple horizontal lines after the fourth day (Oct. 25) indicate when self-correction began. To avoid an emphasis on negative behavior, record all positive actions that you and the child have taken.

 Self-Test

As you begin to use self-correction to deal with a problem behavior, the following guidelines and exercises will assist you. If at all possible, you should do this in consultation with your professional counselor.

Decide on the problem behavior that you wish to eliminate. Select a problem that occurs frequently, preferably several times a day, so that the effect of the self-correction can be detected within the first few days. If a problem occurs infrequently, once per week or less, several weeks must elapse before you will see any obvious change even if the procedure is immediately effective. Under those conditions it is difficult to tell whether or not you are making progress.

Describe the problem behavior you have selected.

_____

_____

_____

_____

(continues)

To change the problem behavior, the disturbance must be corrected; therefore, the exact details of the disturbance must be recorded. Specify the exact nature of the disturbance caused by the behavior you have selected.

_____

_____

_____

_____

_____

In the following space, describe the nature of the simple self-correction you will use. Consider what actions you, as a socially sensitive adult, would take to restore the situation to its previous state if you accidentally committed the problem behavior. Describe the specific actions you will require from someone else for simple self-correction.

_____

_____

_____

Overcorrection is used rather than simple self-correction when the problem behavior is deliberate, frequent, severe, or very annoying. Do you plan to use overcorrection or simple self-correction? Describe the reasons for your decision.

_____

_____

_____

_____

_____

You should keep a record of the occurrence of the problem behaviors. This record should be started several days before you begin the self-correction. Use ordinary lined paper to prepare your recording form. Or use the example form provided below. Fill in the dates in the column on the left, starting with the date on which you will begin recording. Record the problem behavior for at least three days before beginning self-correction.

(continues)

Draw a double line on the recording form at the date when you begin to use self-correction to provide a clear notation of when the new rules begin.

Recording Form

Date	Number of Misbehaviors	Comments

Before you begin the self-correction, examine your record to determine whether the number of episodes is as great as you thought. If it is not, you may wish to reconsider your decision to use self-correction. In the following space, describe what the daily record tells you about the need for action on the problem behavior.

_____

_____

_____

_____

_____

_____

_____

_____

_____

(continues)

Before requiring self-correction from a person, your plans and the reasons for the self-correction should be discussed and agreement should be obtained on the reasonableness of the requirement. For young children, role-playing should be used. For older children, each specific action should be discussed as well as possible complications, distractions, and alternatives if resistance occurs. Describe what you will tell the other person and describe the nature of the role-playing, if it is to be used.

_____

_____

_____

_____

_____

_____

_____

In the following space, describe the results of your discussion (and role-playing). Indicate whether the person agreed with the plan and showed understanding of it by answering your questions about what was to be done. Note especially whether he or she personally described what he or she would do.

_____

_____

_____

_____

_____

_____

_____

(continues)

The self-correction rules should go into effect immediately after the discussion, assuming that positive attention will be provided for positive behaviors.

- Describe what happened when you imposed the self-correction for the first time.
- Did you remind the person to self-correct, or did he or she start doing it spontaneously?
- If the person is a young child, did you stand close by at the time of the reminder and did you use gentle manual guidance?
- Did you watch the correction being carried out?
- Did you praise him or her for initiating and completing the correction?
- Did you insist on total correction?
- Did you offer to help if the person were uncertain, unable, or unwilling to perform the corrective actions?
- Did you require the correction to be performed immediately after the problem behavior occurred?
- If there were a refusal, did you point out the alternative action you would have to take?
- If the person is a child, did he or she become emotional, and if so, did you allow the emotional behavior to disappear before proceeding with the self-correction?
- After the correction, did you praise the child in the presence of other family members?

Use the preceding questions as a guide to describe in detail what happened during this first self-correction requirement:

_____

_____

_____

_____

_____

_____

_____

(continues)

Describe what changes you might make in your own behavior during the next self-correction requirement.

_____

_____

_____

_____

_____

_____

_____

The principle objective of self-correction is to have a person take responsibility for his or her own actions and to avoid anger or punishment. Did you deal with the problem without becoming angry, and did the person accept the self-correction without showing resentment? If not, what actions might you take on future self-corrections to assure a constructive approach by both of you? Describe any emotional behaviors exhibited by either of you, and describe your proposed remedy.

_____

_____

_____

_____

_____

_____

_____

(continues)

Looking at your recording form, how much change has occurred in the problem behaviors as a result of self-correction?

_____

_____

_____

_____

_____

_____

_____

_____

When self-correction has been used successfully for one problem behavior, the success facilitates the use of this strategy for many other problems. Describe what other problem behaviors of the same person you might deal with next by the self-correction requirement.

_____

_____

_____

_____

_____

_____

_____

_____

If you have completed the suggested exercises properly, you should now have a good grasp of the self-correction strategy and should be able to apply it to many everyday problems. The best time to use this strategy, of course, is before a problem becomes severe. By assuming a sense of responsibility for one's actions for slight annoyances, the person will usually self-correct automatically without the need for reminders or special discussions. Equally important, the mastery of this self-correction strategy can provide you with a method of dealing with some of your own feelings of anger at other persons by directing your attention to correcting the situation rather than punishing the person whose behavior offends you. The self-correction approach should benefit both you and the person whom you are requiring to self-correct, and it should do so without feelings of anger in yourself or feelings of guilt in the person you are helping to self-correct.

Combined Use of Positive Practice, Self-Correction, and Overcorrection

The positive practice, self-correction, and overcorrection procedures have been described separately in the previous sections in order to present their distinctively different characteristics. In many situations, each of these procedures may be used to deal with the same problem. The following table illustrates the use of each procedure for several typical problems.

Problem	Self-Correction	Overcorrection	Positive Practice
1. Bedwetting	Clean bed and change pajamas	Remake the bed	Practice going from bed to toilet
2. Slamming a door	Apologize for the noise	Extended apology	Practice closing the door softly
3. Leaving a door or dresser drawer open or a light on	Close the door or drawer, turn the light off	Close any other doors or drawers and turn off other lights	Repeated practice in closing doors and drawers and turning off lights
4. Being left alone at a party by one's partner	Stay together briefly when asked	Stay together for a long period	Partner introduces you to other guests
5. Child stays up after bedtime	Told to go to bed when lateness is noticed	Earlier bedtime the following day	Earlier bedtime for several following days
6. Child spills food on self and floor while eating	Cleans up spillage on self and floor	Cleans up eating area also	Practices eating carefully and slowly

(continues)

Problem	Self-Correction	Overcorrection	Positive Practice
7. Child loses a borrowed item	Replaces the item with another	Conducts an extended search for item and replaces it with a better item	Practices putting items in the appropriate place
8. Driver seen by an officer to exceed the speed limit	Reduces speed to the speed limit	Reduces speed well below speed limit	Practices slow driving; officer requires a driving lesson
9. Person steals an item from a store	Returns item	Pays store an additional amount; court fine	Shops only with another responsible person
10. Girl calls her brother a bad name when he refuses to play with her	Girl apologizes	Girl apologizes and compliments her brother	Girl practices positive requests to her brother
11. Teacher sees a child bullying another child	Tells bully to stop and apologize	Tells bully to stop, apologize, and do the victim some favor	Requires bully to practice being complimentary and making pleasant requests
12. Impulsively broke one's diet by eating a large chocolate bar	Omit equivalent calorie food on next meal	Omit greater number of calories on next meal(s)	Plan each day's meal beforehand; no chocolate purchases
13. Child awakens 15 minutes late	Required to awaken 15 minutes earlier	Required to awaken 30 minutes earlier	Practices setting alarm clock
14. Child hits another child and causes a nosebleed	Require child to assist in needed medical attention	Require child to stop fighting and to assist and reassure the victim	Require child to practice using verbal, not physical, resolution
15. Student makes spelling error on homework report	Correct error on the report	Rewrite each misspelled word several times	A pocket dictionary is provided and its use encouraged and practiced

References and Further Reading

The following are studies using a type of positive practice, self-correction, or overcorrection as the principle procedure or as a component procedure.

Allison, A. G., & Ayllon, T. (1980). Behavioral coaching in the development of skills in football, gymnastics, and tennis. *Journal of Applied Behavior Analysis, 13,* 297–314.

Anderson, G. (1978). Deceleration of severe aggressive behavior via overcorrection and required relaxation. *The Boulder Behaviorist, 6,* 1–2.

Axelrod, S., Brantner, J. P., and Meddock, T. D. (1978). Overcorrection: A review and critical analysis. *The Journal of Special Education, 12,* 367–391.

Azrin, N. H., & Armstrong, P. M. (1973). The "Mini-Meal": A method for teaching eating skills to the profoundly retarded. *Mental Retardation, 11,* 9–13.

Azrin, N. H., & Besalel, V. A. (1980). A parent's guide to bedwetting control: A step-by-step method. New York: Simon & Schuster.

Azrin, N. H., & Foxx, R. M. (1971). A rapid method of toilet training the institutionalized retarded. *Journal of Applied Behavior Analysis, 4,* 89–99.

Azrin, N. H., & Foxx, R. M. (1974). *Toilet training in less than a day.* New York: Simon & Schuster.

Azrin, N. H., Gottlieb, L., Hughart, L., Wesolowski, M. D., & Rahn, T. (1975). Eliminating self-injurious behavior by educative procedures. *Behavior Research and Therapy, 13,* 101–111.

Azrin, N. H., Hontos, P. T., & Besalel-Azrin, V. (1979). Elimination of enuresis without a conditioning apparatus: An extension by office instruction of the child and parents. *Behavior Therapy, 10,* 14–19.

Azrin, N. H., Kaplan, S. J., & Foxx, R. M. (1973). Autism reversal: Eliminating stereotyped self-stimulation of retarded individuals. *American Journal of Mental Deficiency, 78,* 241–248.

Azrin, N. H., & Nunn, R. G. (1973). Habit reversal: A method of eliminating nervous habits and tics. *Behavior Research and Therapy, 11,* 619–628.

Azrin, N. H., & Nunn, R. G. (1974). A rapid method of eliminating stuttering by a regulated breathing approach. *Behavior Research and Therapy, 12,* 279–286.

Azrin, N. H., & Nunn, R. G. (1977). Habit control: Stuttering, nail biting, and other nervous habits. New York: Simon & Schuster.

Azrin, N. H., Nunn, R. G., and Frantz, S. E. (1979). Comparison of regulated-breathing vs. abbreviated desensitization on reported stuttering episodes. *Journal of Speech and Hearing Disorders, 44,* 331–339.

Azrin, N. H., Nunn, R. G., & Frantz, S. E. (1980). Habit reversal treatment of thumbsucking. *Behavior Research and Therapy, 18,* 395–399.

Azrin, N. H., Nunn, R. G., & Frantz, S. E. (1980). Habit reversal vs. negative practice treatment of nail biting. *Behavior Research and Therapy, 18,* 281–285.

Azrin, N. H., Nunn, R. G., & Frantz, S. E. (1980). Habit reversal vs. negative practice treatment of nervous tics. *Behavior Therapy, 11,* 169–178.

Azrin, N. H., Nunn, R. G., & Frantz, S. E. (1980). Treatment of trichotillomania (hairpulling): A comparative study of habit reversal and negative practice training. *Journal of Behavior Therapy and Experimental Psychiatry, 11*, 13–20.

Azrin, N. H., & Powers, M. A. (1975). Eliminating classroom disturbances of emotionally disturbed children by positive practice procedures. *Behavior Therapy, 6*, 525–534.

Azrin, N. H., Sneed, T. J., & Foxx, R. M. (1973). Dry bed: A rapid method of eliminating bedwetting (enuresis) of the retarded. *Behavior Research and Therapy, 11*, 427–434.

Azrin, N. H., Sneed, T. J., & Foxx, R. M. (1974). Dry-bed training: Rapid elimination of childhood enuresis. *Behavior Research and Therapy, 12*, 147–156.

Azrin, N. H., & Thienes, P. M. (1978). Rapid elimination of enuresis by intensive learning without a conditioning apparatus. *Behavior Therapy, 9*, 342–354.

Azrin, N. H., & Wesolowski, M. D. (1974). Theft reversal: An overcorrection procedure for eliminating stealing by retarded persons. *Journal of Applied Behavior Analysis, 7*, 577–581.

Azrin, N. H., & Wesolowski, M. D. (1975). Eliminating habitual vomiting in a retarded adult by positive practice and self-correction. *Journal of Behavior Therapy and Experimental Psychiatry, 6*, 145–148.

Azrin, N. H., & Wesolowski, M. D. (1975). The use of positive practice to eliminate persistent floor sprawling by profoundly retarded persons. *Behavior Therapy, 6*, 627–631.

Azrin, N. H., & Wesolowski, M. D. (1980). A reinforcement interruption method of eliminating behavioral sterotypy of profoundly retarded persons. *Behavior Research and Therapy, 18*, 113–119.

Azrin, V. B., Azrin, N. H., & Armstrong, P. M. (1977). The student-oriented classroom: A method of improving student conduct and satisfaction. *Behavior Therapy, 8*, 193–204.

Barmann, B. C. (1979). The use of overcorrection with artificial fingernail biting. *Mental Retardation, 17*, 309–311.

Barton, E. J., & Osborne, J. G. (1978). The development of classroom sharing by a teacher using positive practice. *Behavior Modification, 2*, 231–250.

Bernstein, P. H., Hamilton, S. B., and Quevillon, R. P. (1977). Behavior modification by long distance. *Behavior Modification, 1*, 369–380.

Bernstein, P. H., Hamilton, S. B., & Quevillon, R. P. (1977). Behavior modification by long-distance: Demonstration of functional control over disruptive behavior in a rural classroom setting. *Behavior Modification, 1*, 369–380.

Besalel, V. A., and Azrin, N. H. (1981). The reduction of parent–youth problems by reciprocity counseling. *Behavior Research and Therapy, 19*, 297–301.

Basalel, V. A., Azrin, N. H., & Thienes-Hontos, P. (1980). Evaluation of a parent's manual for training enuretic children. *Behavior Research and Therapy, 18*, 358–360.

Bitgood, S. C., Crowe, M. J., Suarez, Y., & Peters, R. D. (1980). Immobilization: Effects and side effects on stereotyped behavior in children. *Behavior Modification, 4*, 187–208.

Carey, R. G., & Bucher, B. (1981). Identifying the educative and suppressive effects of positive practice and restitutional overcorrection. *Journal of Applied Behavior Analysis, 14*, 71–80.

Carey, R. G., & Bucher, B. D. (1983). Positive practice overcorrection: The effects of duration of positive practice on acquisition and response reduction. *Journal of Applied Behavior Analysis, 16*, 101–109.

Carey, R. G., & Bucher, B. D. (1986). Positive practice overcorrection: Effects of reinforcing correct performance. *Behavior Modification, 10*, 73–92.

Carroll, S. W., Sloop, E. W., Mutter, S., & Prince, L. P. (1979). The elimination of chronic clothes ripping in retarded people through a combination of procedures. *Mental Retardation, 16,* 246–249.

Close, D. W., Irvin, L. K., Prehm, H. J., & Taylor, V. E. (1978). Systematic correction procedures in vocational skill training of severely retarded individuals. *American Journal of Mental Deficiency, 83,* 270–275.

DeCatanzaro, D. A., & Baldwin, G. (1978). Effective treatment of self-injurious behavior through a forced arm exercise. *American Journal of Mental Deficiency, 82,* 433–439.

Denny, M. (1980). Reducing self-stimulatory behavior of mentally retarded persons by alternative positive practice. *American Journal of Mental Deficiency, 84,* 610–615.

Epstein, L. H., Doke, L. A., Sajwaj, T. E., Sorrell, S., & Rimmer, B. (1974). Generality and side effects of overcorrection. *Journal of Applied Behavior Analysis, 7,* 385–390.

Fitterling, M., & Ayllon, T. (1983). Behavioral coaching in classical ballet. *Behavior Modification, 7,* 350–352.

Foxx, R. M. (1976). Increasing a mildly retarded woman's attendance at self-help classes by overcorrection and instruction. *Behavior Therapy, 7,* 390–396.

Foxx, R. M. (1976). The use of overcorrection to eliminate the public disrobing (stripping) of retarded women. *Behavior Research and Therapy, 14,* 53–61.

Foxx, R. M. (1977). Attention training: The use of overcorrection avoidance to increase the eye contact of autistic and retarded children. *Journal of Applied Behavior Analysis, 10,* 488–499.

Foxx, R. M., & Azrin, N. H. (1972). Restitution: A method of eliminating aggressive-disruptive behavior of retarded and brain damaged patients. *Behavior Research and Therapy, 10,* 15–27.

Foxx, R. M., & Azrin, N. H. (1973). The elimination of autistic self-stimulatory behavior by overcorrection. *Journal of Applied Behavior Analysis, 6,* 1–14.

Foxx, R. M., & Azrin, N. H. (1973). Dry pants: A rapid method of toilet training children. *Behavior Research and Therapy, 11,* 435–442.

Foxx, R. M., & Azrin, N. H. (1973). Toilet training the retarded: A rapid program for day and nighttime independent training. Champaign, IL: Research Press Co.

Foxx, R. M., & Bechtel, D. R. (1982). Overcorrection. *Progress in Behavior Modification, 13,* 227–228.

Foxx, R. M., & Bechtel, D. R. (1983). Overcorrection: A review and analysis. In S. Axelrod & J. Apsche (Eds.), *The effects of punishment on human behavior* (pp. 133–220). New York: Academic Press.

Foxx, R. M., & Jones, J. R. (1978). A remediation program for increasing the spelling achievement of elementary and junior high school students. *Behavior Modification, 2,* 211–230.

Foxx, R. M., & Livesay, J. (1984). Maintenance of response suppression following overcorrection: A 10-year retrospective of eight cases. *Analysis and Intervention in Developmental Disabilities, 4,* 65–79.

Foxx, R. M., & Martin, E. D. (1975). Treatment of scavenging behavior (coprophagy and pica) by overcorrection. *Behavior Research and Therapy, 13,* 153–162.

Freeman, B. J., Moss, D., Somerset, T., and Ritvo, E. R. (1977). Thumbsucking in an autistic child overcome by overcorrection. *Journal of Behavior Therapy and Experimental Psychiatry, 8,* 211–212.

Harris, S. L., & Ersner-Hershfield, R. (1978). The behavioral suppression of seriously disruptive behavior in psychotic and retarded patients: A review of punishment and its alternatives. *Psychological Bulletin, 85,* 1352–1375.

Harris, S. L., & Romanczyk, R. G. (1976). Treating self-injurious behavior of a retarded child by overcorrection. *Behavior Therapy, 7,* 235–239.

Harris, S. L., & Wolchik, S. A. (1979). Suppression of self-stimulation: Three alternative strategies. *Journal of Applied Behavior Analysis, 12,* 185–198.

Judkins, J. D. (1976). Overcorrection procedures with the institutionalized retarded: An evaluative review. *Mental Retardation Bulletin, 4,* 98–110.

Kazdin, A. E., French, N. H., & Sherick, R. B. (1981). Acceptability of alternative treatments for children: Evaluations by inpatient children, parents, and staff. *Journal of Consulting and Clinical Psychology, 49,* 900–907.

Luiselli, J. K., Helfen, C. S., Pemberton, B. W., & Reisman, J. (1977). The elimination of a child's in-class masturbation by overcorrection and reinforcement. *Journal of Behavior Therapy and Experimental Psychiatry, 8,* 201–204.

Marholin, D., II, Luiselli, J. K., and Townsend, N. M. (1980). Overcorrection: An examination of its rationale and treatment effectiveness. In M. Hersen, R. M. Eisler, and P. M. Miller (Eds.). *Progress in Behavior Modification: Vol. 9* (pp. 49–80). New York: Academic Press.

Marholin, D., & Townsend, N. M. (1978). An experimental analysis of side effects and response maintenance of a modified overcorrection procedure. *Behavior Therapy, 9,* 383–390.

Matson, J. L., Horne, A. M., Ollendick, D. G., & Ollendick, T. H. (1979). Overcorrection: A further evaluation of restitution and positive practice. *Journal of Behavior Therapy and Experimental Psychiatry, 10,* 295–298.

Matson, J. L., & Stephens, R. M. (1977). Overcorrection of aggressive behavior in a chronic psychiatric patient. *Behavior Modification, 1,* 559–564.

Matson, J. L., Stephens, R. M., & Home, A. M. (1978). Overcorrection and extinction-reinforcement as rapid methods of eliminating the disruptive behaviors of relatively normal children. *Behavioral Engineering, 4,* 89–94.

Matson, J. L., Stephens, R. M., and Smith, C. (1978). Treatment of self-injurious behavior with overcorrection. *Journal of Mental Deficiency Research, 22,* 175–178.

Matson, J. L., & Taras, M. E. (1989). A 20-year review of punishment and alternative methods to treat problem behaviors in developmentally delayed persons. *Research in Developmental Disabilities, 10,* 85–104.

McGrath, P., Marshall, P. G., & Prior, K. (1979). A comprehensive treatment program for a fire setting child. *Journal of Behavior Therapy and Experimental Psychiatry, 10,* 69–72.

Miltenberger, R. G., & Fuqua, R. W. (1981). Overcorrection: A review and critical analysis. *The Behavior Analyst, 4,* 123–141.

Nunn, R. G., Azrin, N. H. (1976). Eliminating nail biting by the habit-reversal procedure. *Behavior Research and Therapy, 14,* 65–67.

Ollendick, T. H., Matson, J. L., Esveldt-Dawson, K., & Shapiro, E. S. (1980). Increasing spelling achievement: An analysis of treatment procedures utilizing an alternating treatments design. *Journal of Applied Behavior Analysis, 13,* 645–654.

Osborne, J. G. (1976). Overcorrection and behavior therapy: A reply to Hobbs. *Rehabilitation Psychology, 23,* 13–31.

Polvinale, R. A., and Lutzker, J. R. (1980). Elimination of assaultive and inappropriate sexual behavior by reinforcement and social-restitution. *Mental Retardation, 18,* 27–30.

Porterfield, J. K., Herbert-Jackson, E., & Risley, T. (1976). Contingent observation: An effective and acceptable procedure for reducing disruptive behaviors of young children in group settings. *Journal of Applied Behavior Analysis, 9,* 55–64.

Rasmussen, P. R. (1973). *An alternative procedure for eliminating a child's undesirable behavior using the mother as therapist: A case study.* Unpublished master's thesis, Southern Illinois University, Carbondale, IL.

Roberts, P., Iwata, B. A., McSween, T. E., & Desmond, E. F., Jr. (1979). An analysis of overcorrection movements. *American Journal of Mental Deficiency, 83,* 588–594.

Singh, N. N. (1987). Overcorrection of oral reading errors. A comparison of individual and group-training formats. *Behavior Modification, 11,* 165–181.

Singh, N. N., & Singh, J. (1986). Increasing oral reading proficiency. A comparative analysis of drill and positive practice overcorrection procedures. *Behavior Modification, 10,* 115–130.

Singh, N. N., Singh, J., & Winton, A. S. W. (1984). Positive practice overcorrection of oral reading errors. *Behavior Modification, 8,* 23–37.

Stewart, C. A., & Singh, N. N. (1986). Overcorrection of spelling deficits in mentally retarded persons. *Behavior Modification, 10,* 355–365.

Webster, D. R., & Azrin, N. H. (1973). Required relaxation: A method of inhibiting agitative-disruptive behavior of retardates. *Behavior Research and Therapy, 11,* 67–78.

Wells, K. C., Forehand, R., Hickey, K., & Green, K. D. (1977). Effects of a procedure derived from the overcorrection principle on manipulated and nonmanipulated behavior. *Journal of Applied Behavior Analysis, 10,* 679–687.